Puffling Patrol

For Ruth and her husband, Siggi; Dáni and Erna;
and all the children of Heimaey.

Special thanks to Erpur and Kristján.

Lee & Low Books Inc.
New York

Puffling Patrol

Caldecott Honor Winners
Ted and Betsy Lewin

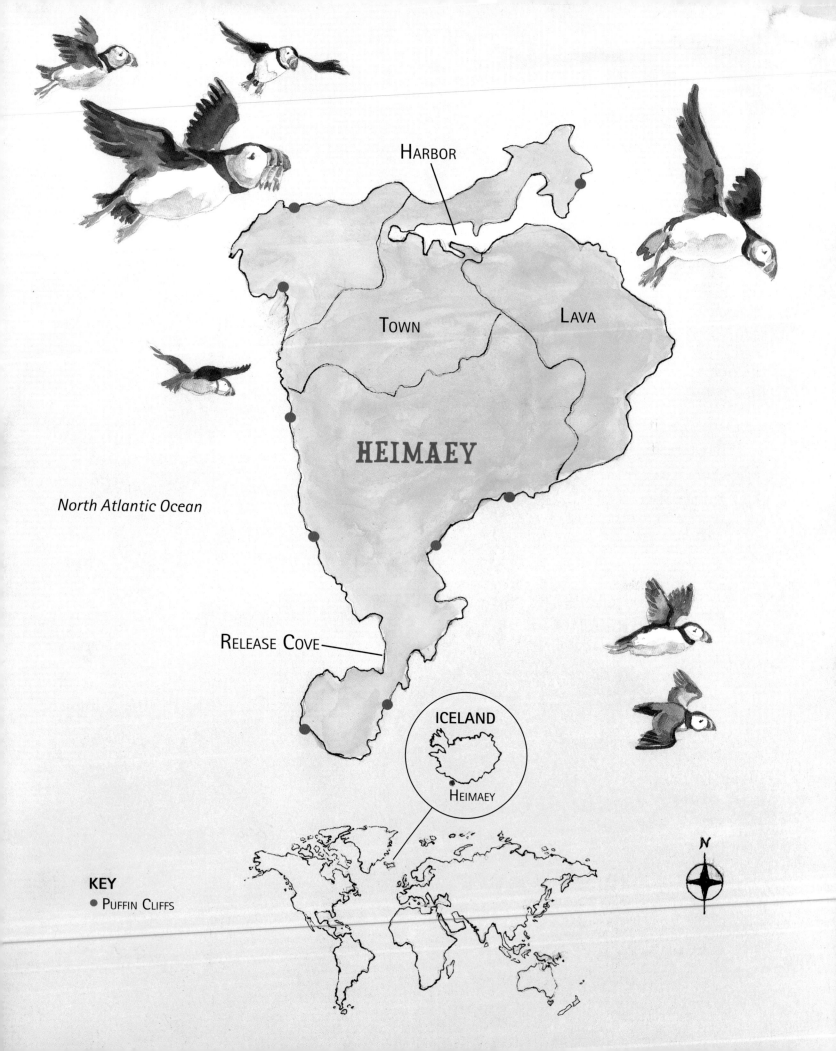

HARBOR

TOWN

LAVA

HEIMAEY

North Atlantic Ocean

RELEASE COVE

ICELAND

HEIMAEY

KEY
● PUFFIN CLIFFS

N

Off the southern coast of Iceland lies a stretch of rugged volcanic islands called Vestmannaeyjar, the Westman Islands. Nineteen small, rocky islands and stacks rise out of the cold North Atlantic Ocean. The newest island, Surtsey, arose from the sea in 1963, the result of a series of underwater eruptions. The largest island, Heimaey, is the only one inhabited by people. Its population of about four thousand three hundred residents live in the shadow of the island's towering cliffs. Most people catch fish for a living, but their real love is for puffins, the small, chunky, black-and-white seabirds.

Every April, the Westman Islands become home to hundreds of thousands of puffins, one of the largest puffin colonies in the world. The puffins return to the islands to lay eggs and raise their chicks in burrows dug into the soil on the cliffs. By August, the young puffins, called pufflings, are ready to leave their burrows. In the dark of night, they fly off the cliffs and head for the sea. But some pufflings on Heimaey, confused by the lights of the town, flutter down onto the streets instead of flying out to sea. Their wings are not strong enough for them to take off again from the flat surfaces of the streets. So when it starts "raining pufflings" in town, it is time for the children of The Puffling Patrol to begin their rescue mission. This yearly event is what we have come to Heimaey to see.

Jack & Betsy

It is the end of August. Soon the adult puffins will be gone to spend the winter in the cold northern seas. The pufflings in the dark burrows will then be on their own.

From our airplane window we see the mist-shrouded Westman Islands jutting up from the sea as we approach Heimaey. Ruth, our guide, meets us at the airport. She whisks us away to the dock in the harbor, where a research team is about to leave for the last survey of the puffin burrows before the weather turns stormy.

"This is a great chance to see puffins up close on the water," says Ruth.

Twenty minutes later we crowd into a Zodiac boat with four team members, all of us wearing our bulky orange life vests. We barely fit into the small, inflatable boat. Holding onto ropes along the sides of the Zodiac, we roar out of the harbor and into the open sea, heading for one of the smaller islands we saw from the plane. We slam into huge, rolling waves. It feels as if we are riding a bucking bronco.

Erpur, from the South Iceland Nature Centre, is the team leader. Over the din of the boat's motor he yells to us, "Are you cold and miserable yet?"

"No. We're fine," we say, shivering.

Groups of puffins, called rafts, ride the waves like toy ducks. We pull into a cove. With the steep cliffs and caves and crashing seas, it looks as if there is no place to land. Erpur guns the motor, and the boat lurches in the waves and up onto the rocks. The researchers leap out onto the slippery rocks as the boat slides back into the sea. It is a tricky, dangerous landing.

Once ashore, the researchers climb up the high cliffs toward the puffins' burrows. We wait, bobbing in the surf with Erpur, who tells us about their work.

Erpur and his team have been monitoring the puffin burrows, which are marked with metal plates on stakes. We watch the researchers through binoculars. They use a special camera on a long cable to look in the burrows to see if there is an egg or a chick inside. The researchers visit each burrow many times during the summer to check how well the chicks are growing.

There is a shortage of sand eels, the puffins' main food, Erpur tells us. For the past several years, the puffins' food supply has been decreasing. This may be happening because the sea is getting warmer. When it is time for the adult birds to leave the island, some of the pufflings in the burrows may still be undersized because the adults were not able to bring them enough food.

After the researchers come down from the cliffs, getting back into the Zodiac is even more dangerous than getting out. They dive headfirst into the boat, tumbling over one another and almost tossing us overboard.

On the return trip to Heimaey we pass the island of Brandur. Suddenly the sky is filled with gannets, large white birds with 6-foot (1.8-meter) wingspans, soaring and swooping gracefully. More gannets, with their black chicks, perch on the sheer cliffs of this rocky island. The cliffs are stained white with their droppings, as if someone has tossed white paint on the rocks.

Ruth meets us at the dock. As soon as we recover our land legs, she takes us to meet Kristján, the director of the Natural History Museum in town. We find him behind the scenes of the big aquarium tanks that are filled with local sea life, including wolffish, Icelandic lobsters, and sea anemones.

Kristján is watching over the first rescued puffling of the year, found by the police the night before. It is still covered with a soft, fluffy coat of down and is too young to be on its own. The puffling sits in a cardboard box begging for food.

Helping to feed the puffling are Dáni and Erna, eight-year-old twins. Dáni and his sister love caring for young puffins. The children are part of The Puffling Patrol. They are eagerly waiting for night to come so they can rescue pufflings that have flown the wrong way and landed in town. If the little birds are not found quickly, they could be snatched up by cats or dogs, or run over by cars or trucks.

"Would you like to hold the puffling?" Kristján asks us. We take turns cradling the bird in our hands. It seems so helpless. We wonder how it could possibly ever survive out at sea.

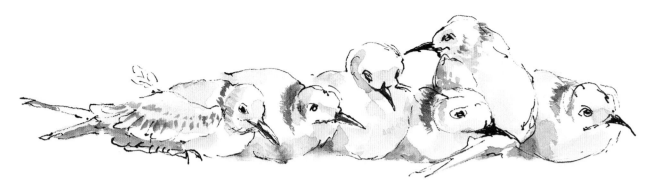

We set out for Ruth's backyard, stopping along the way to buy Erna and Dáni cups of ice cream. Ruth has six kittiwake chicks in her yard. She has been caring for the little birds for six weeks, and they are just about ready to fly off.

Dáni sets his cup on the table. Immediately the birds fly over and greedily jam their bills into the ice cream.

After the chicks finish their snack, the children joyously toss the young birds into the air so they can exercise their wings.

Soon a boy appears holding a cardboard box with a fulmar inside. Fulmars have a nasty habit of spitting foul-smelling fish oil from their stomachs when they are frightened. The boy is happy to hand over the bird to Ruth.

Next a girl arrives with another kittiwake. Then a fisherman calls to say he has found a puffling. He is keeping it in his shed. It seems that everyone on the island rescues and cares for the seabirds!

In the afternoon we go with Dáni and Erna
to the grocery store to get some cardboard boxes
for our evening patrol.

"Have you found a puffling?" asks the clerk.

"Not yet. Tonight, we hope," says Erna.

The children return home for dinner, and we go back
to Ruth's house. The children join us later with their father.

By ten o'clock it has gotten dark enough to head out. Erna
and Dáni gather the boxes and their flashlights. The children are
allowed to stay up late because rescuing pufflings is part of their
duty as members of The Puffling Patrol.

It is pouring outside when we leave Ruth's house. The rain is blowing sideways. We crowd into the car with Erna, Dáni, and their father. The children cannot wait to find their first puffling.

We drive slowly through the streets, peering into the light from the car's headlights for any signs of pufflings.

Suddenly Dáni yells, "STOP!" His father pulls over and Dáni leaps from the car, his flashlight beam stabbing the darkness. We jump out into the soaking rain too, eager to see him discover a puffling. But what caught Dáni's eye is only a piece of paper blowing in the wind.

"Dáni has eagle eyes," the children's father tells us. "Last year he rescued twenty-seven pufflings in one night."

At last "Eagle Eyes" spots something. He and Erna rush over and find a frightened puffling. They catch the bird in a circle of light from their flashlights.

The puffling does not move as Erna and Dáni approach. After a few moments they tenderly lift the little bird and stroke its head, then lower it into a cardboard box.

After placing the box in their father's car, the children continue searching for pufflings. But they do not come across any more.

"The pufflings really haven't started leaving their burrows yet or we'd see them gliding down everywhere," the children's father explains.

Dáni and Erna take their rescued puffling home for the night. Erna keeps the little bird close so it will stay warm. Dáni comes over to say good night to them. Before Erna goes to sleep she will put the puffling back in its box for the night.

We say good night too and return to our hotel. We are exhausted, but thrilled that we have just been on our first Puffling Patrol.

The next day we go back to the Natural History Museum
with Ruth, Erna, and Dáni. We watch as the children's puffling
is measured and weighed. The museum staff then
adds this information to their records, which
are used to keep track of the pufflings that are
rescued each year.

Ruth tells us that pufflings must weigh at least
10.6 ounces (300 grams), about the weight of
two baseballs, to survive on their own. Dáni
and Erna are happy that the bird they
rescued weighs enough to be released
right away.

Kristján shows us the other pufflings that were brought in last night. They are all in good shape and big enough to be sent out to sea.

The children take the boxes of pufflings and place them in Ruth's truck. We head for a cove at the other end of the island. The pufflings are scratching around and flapping their wings in the boxes. We think they must be anxious to get into the water.

Dáni and Erna are so excited! At the cove they carefully carry the boxes across the beach to the water's edge.

The children open the boxes, and the pufflings peer up at their smiling faces. Erna and Dáni each reach into a box and lift out a little bird.

The children gently hold their precious charges.
It is time to release the pufflings and send
them out to sea.

"Good luck," whispers Erna.
"Be careful, little one."

Erna and Dáni hold up their pufflings,
letting them flap their wings. The birds
are getting ready to fly.

Then the children begin to count.

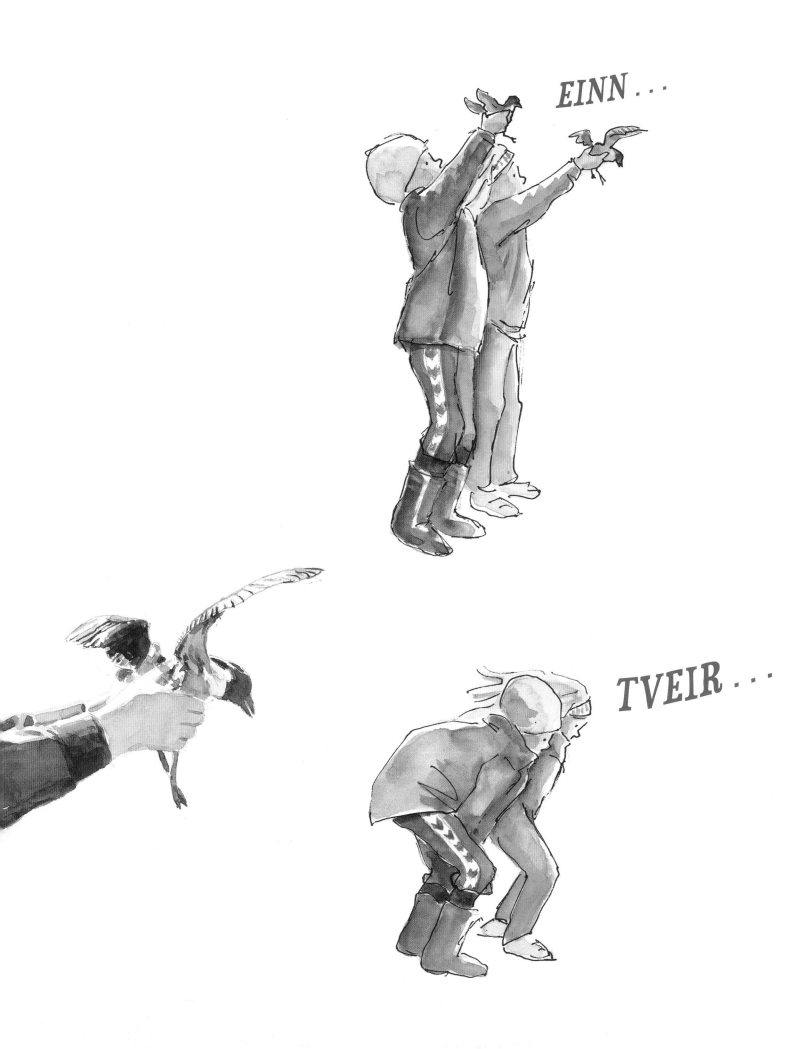

... ÞRÍR!

The pufflings glide down, hit the water, and disappear beneath the surface.

"They sank!" we gasp.

Ruth laughs. "The first thing the pufflings do when they hit the water is dive," she explains. "Even though they've never been in the water before, they know exactly what to do."

Just then the pufflings pop back up.

"*Bless, bless,*" Dáni and Erna yell. "Good-bye, good-bye."

We all watch as the pufflings confidently paddle off in the cold North Atlantic Ocean. Then the children release the other birds we have brought to the cove.

The sea will be the puffins' home for the next two years. If all goes well, they will return to Heimaey as adults and raise their own chicks. When they do, Erna and Dáni, along with the rest of The Puffling Patrol, will be ready with their flashlights and cardboard boxes to help rescue the pufflings that land in town.

Atlantic Puffin Facts

An adult Atlantic puffin is about 10 to 12 inches (25 to 30.5 centimeters) tall and weighs about 17.5 ounces (496 grams). The male puffin is slightly larger than the female.

Atlantic puffins live to be about twenty to twenty-five years old in the wild. They are found in the North Atlantic Ocean from Maine in the United States to Canada, Greenland, Iceland, the United Kingdom, Norway, and northwestern France.

Male and female puffins look identical. They have black and white feathers and large, brightly colored bills. They are sometimes called "clowns of the sea" or "sea parrots" because of their colorful appearance.

Puffins spend the winter at sea, then come ashore on rocky cliffs to breed in the spring. In winter, a puffin's bill fades to gray. In spring, the bill becomes colorful again, which may help attract a mate during breeding season. The bill also increases in size each year.

Puffins begin to pair up when they are about five years old. Once on land, a pair bonds by "billing," rubbing their bills together. Puffins often stay together for life and return to the same burrow year after year.

Puffins use their thick bills to dig a burrow, then kick out the dirt with their feet. A burrow is commonly about 5 feet (1.5 meters) long.

A female lays one egg, and both the male and female take turns incubating it. The chick hatches in about forty-two days. The adults also take turns feeding their chick four to ten times a day with small fish from the sea. During the time a puffling is in the burrow, it may eat as many as two thousand fish. After six weeks, the adults stop bringing their puffling food and leave for the winter. The puffling is then completely on its own. A week later, the young bird ventures out of the burrow.

2 DAYS   1 WEEK   2 MONTHS   ADULT

Puffin chicks make peeping noises to tell their parents they are hungry. Adult puffins communicate with loud, growling calls.

XXX

Adult puffins also communicate with body movements. Walking quickly with the head lowered means a puffin poses no threat to others, and friendliness is indicated by exaggerated foot stomping. Aggression is shown by "gaping," puffing up the body to look bigger and opening the wings and bill slightly. When it is time for the adults to fly to the sea for the night, they jerk up their heads as a signal to others that it is time to go.

XXX

Although they are birds, puffins live most of their lives in the sea. They swim using their wings to paddle and their webbed feet to steer.

XXX

Puffins' chunky bodies and short wings make it difficult for them to take off from the flat surface of the water on windless days. They often need a long "run" along the water to get up in the air. Once in the air, they flap their wings about six hundred times a minute and speed along at about 50 miles (80 kilometers) an hour.

Puffins can dive as deep as 200 feet (61 meters) to hunt. They can stay underwater for one minute or more, but usually a dive lasts only 20 to 30 seconds. Using their tongues to hold sand eels and other small fish against ridges on the roofs of their mouths, puffins can carry up to sixty-two tiny fish in their bills at one time.

XXX

Scientists are not sure exactly how puffin couples find their way back to their home islands and their burrows each spring. The birds may use sounds, smells, visual reference points, or even the stars as guides.

The Volcano of 1973

At around 2 a.m. on January 23, 1973, a fissure about 1 mile (1.6 kilometers) long opened along the eastern side of Heimaey. The entire length of the fissure began erupting, spewing forth hot ash, gas, rocks, and lava. Luckily most of the island's fishing fleet was in the harbor due to bad weather the day before. Within six hours, everyone on the island was evacuated by boat or airplane to the mainland of Iceland. A small crew of emergency workers stayed behind to save what they could.

By February, the lava flow threatened to close off the town's harbor, an important fishing port. Firefighters decided to pump cold seawater onto the lava to try to slow it down. This method turned out to be effective, and the U.S. Army Corps of Engineers soon lent the firefighters more powerful pumps. For the next few months firefighters sprayed seawater onto the hot lava. Finally an outer crust formed, causing the lava to flow away from the harbor and into the sea.

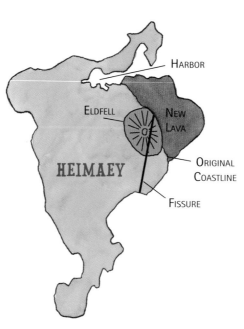

The eruption was declared officially ended five months later, on July 3. Four hundred forty homes had been buried under lava or destroyed by fire, and another four hundred homes were damaged. About 1.65 million tons (1.5 million metric tons) of ash had fallen on the town in Heimaey. When the townspeople returned, they found that the island was 0.85 square mile (2.2 square kilometers) larger. They set to work digging out from under the tons of ash and rebuilding.

Today Heimaey's beautiful harbor and neat, colorful rows of houses sparkle in the sun. A high wall of black lava sits where it hardened, one crushed house still visible. The volcano is 660 feet (200 meters) high. The people of Heimaey named it Eldfell, or Fire Mountain. In some places the ground of Eldfell is still hot enough slightly below the surface for islanders to bake bread on the lava.

Vestmannaeyjar's Puffins Today

In recent years the number of puffin chicks that survive on the Westman Islands has been declining. The reason for this is the diminishing supply of sand eels, on which puffins feed. There are various theories about what is causing the decrease in sand eels. "The ocean temperature has increased," says Erpur, "and some [scientists] believe that bacteria could have emerged after a certain temperature threshold. . . . But many things are happening simultaneously in the ocean here, and it appears to be an ecosystem shift." The situation of puffins that have been monitored in northern Iceland is better due to the existence of a food source called capelin, small fish that live in the colder water.

Because fewer puffin chicks on Heimaey are surviving, the annual puffling rescue has been affected. In 2007, about 1,600 pufflings were rescued by The Puffling Patrol. The year we visited, 2008, about 160 were found in town. In 2010, only 10 pufflings were rescued. There are still more than 800,000 breeding pairs of puffins on the island, and we can only hope that the situation will change for the better.

For More Information About Puffins

"Atlantic Puffins." National Geographic Kids. http://kids.nationalgeographic.com/kids/animals/creaturefeature/atlanticpuffin/.

Bailer, Darice. *Puffin's Homecoming: The Story of an Atlantic Puffin*. Norwalk, CT: Soundprints, 1993.

Kress, Stephen W. *Project Puffin: How We Brought Puffins Back to Egg Rock*. Gardiner, ME: Tilbury House, 2003.

McMillan, Bruce. Bruce's Puffin Page. http://www.brucemcmillan.com/FRB_PuffinPage.html.

———. *Nights of the Pufflings*. New York: Houghton Mifflin, 1995.

Quinlan, Susan E. *Puffins*. Minneapolis, MN: Carolrhoda Books, 1998.

Squire, Ann O. *Puffins: A True Book*. Danbury, CT: Children's Press, 2006.

Zecca, Katherine. *A Puffin's Year*. Rockport, ME: Down East Books, 2007.

Glossary and Pronunciation Guide

The pronunciations provided for Icelandic words and names are the best approximations available for English speakers.

aquarium (uh-KWER-ee-uhm): glass container where water animals and plants are kept; building in which these animals and plants are kept and exhibited

bill (bil): hard, horny part of a bird's mouth; beak of a bird

bless (blehss): Icelandic for "good-bye"

Brandur (BRAN-dur): island in the Westman Islands, Iceland

breed (breed): to produce young animals

burrow (BUR-oh): hole in the ground that an animal makes to live in or for safety

capelin (KAH-puh-len): small fish of the smelt family found in northern oceans

chick (chik): newly hatched or very young bird

Dáni (DAN-ee): male Icelandic name

down (doun): covering of soft, fluffy feathers

ecosystem (EK-oh-sis-tuhm *or* EE-koh-sis-tuhm): community of living things interacting with its environment

einn (ayt): Icelandic for "one"

Eldfell (ELD-fel): Fire Mountain; volcano on Heimaey, formed in 1973

Erna (ER-nah): female Icelandic name

Erpur (ER-purr): male Icelandic name

erupt (i-RUHPT): to burst forth or break through a surface

fissure (FISH-er): long, narrow opening or crack

fulmar (FUL-mer *or* FUL-mar): heavy, gray, gull-like seabird; lives in Arctic regions

gannet (GAH-net): large white bird with long, pointed wings, black wing tips, and long bill

Heimaey (HAY-mah-ay): largest island in the Westman Islands, Iceland; the only island on which people live

Iceland (EYESS-luhnd): island country in the North Atlantic Ocean; includes several smaller islands

incubate (IN-kyuh-bate): to sit on eggs so they will be kept warm and will hatch

inhabit (in-HAH-bit): to live in a place; to have a home in a place

kittiwake (KIT-ee-wayk): small, gray-and-white gull found in northern regions; builds its nest on cliffs and spends the winter in the sea (ocean)

Kristján (KRISS-tjown): male Icelandic name

land legs (land legz): ability to regain a sense of balance while walking on land after spending time on a boat

lava (LAH-vuh): hot, liquid rock that pours from a volcano; rock formed when this liquid has cooled and hardened

lobster (LOB-stur): sea creature with a hard shell and five pairs of legs

mate (mate): male or female of a pair of animals

þrír (THRR-ear): Icelandic for "three"

puffin (PUH-fen *or* PUHF-in): black-and-white seabird with a large, colorful bill that lives in northern regions

puffling (PUH-fling *or* PUHF-ling): young puffin

raft (raft): group of puffins on water

sand eel (sand eel): small, slender fish with a long head and sharply pointed nose

sea anemone (see uh-NEH-muh-nee): small sea animal with a tube-shaped body and a mouth opening surrounded by brightly colored tentacles

seabird (SEE-berd): bird that lives on or near the sea (ocean)

stack (stak): column of rock standing in the sea remaining after a cliff has been worn away by waves

Surtsey (SURT-see): newest island in the Westman Islands, Iceland

tveir (TV-ay): Icelandic for "two"

Vestmannaeyjar (VEST-mannah-ir): Icelandic for "Westman Islands"

volcano (vol-KAY-noh): mountain with openings through which lava, ash, rocks, and gas erupt, usually violently

Westman Islands (WESS-mun EYE-luhnds): group of small islands off the southern coast of Iceland

wolffish (WULF-fish): large, bony fish with strong teeth

Zodiac (ZOH-dee-ak): inflatable boat; Zodiac® is a brand of inflatable boats, life rafts, and water safety equipment

Authors' Sources

This story is based on actual events that took place on Heimaey, Westman Islands, Iceland, in August 2008. Much of the research was conducted while the authors were visiting the Westman Islands and encompasses their primary experiences and observations, and conversations with guides and experts there, including Erpur Snær Hansen, Divisional Manager of Ecological Research at the South Iceland Nature Centre, Heimaey, Iceland; Kristján Egilsson, retired Director of the Natural History Museum, Heimaey, Iceland; and Ruth Zohlen, their guide on Heimaey.

Harris, M. P. *The Puffin*. Calton, UK: T. & A. D. Poyser Ltd., 1984.

Martin, Lynne. *Puffin: Bird of the Open Seas*. New York: William Morrow and Company, 1976.

"Project Puffin: Seabird Restoration Program." Audubon. http://projectpuffin.org/.

The official name of the puffling rescue is The Puffling Patrol with Bruce the Rescuer/*Psyjueftirlitið með Brúsa Bjargfasta*, in honor of Bruce McMillan and his photo-illustrated children's book *Nights of the Pufflings*, which chronicled the event and spread the news of this unique local puffling rescue far beyond Iceland's shores.

LEE & LOW BOOKS Inc., 95 Madison Avenue, New York, NY 10016, leeandlow.com
Manufactured in China by Jade Productions, February 2012
Book design by Susan and David Neuhaus/NeuStudio
Book production by The Kids at Our House
The text is set in 12.5-point Rotis San Serif.
The full-spread illustrations are rendered in watercolor on Strathmore Bristol board.
The field sketches are rendered in pen and ink, and watercolor.
First Edition   10 9 8 7 6 5 4 3 2 1

Library of Congress Cataloging-in-Publication Data
Lewin, Ted.
Puffling patrol / Ted and Betsy Lewin.
   p. cm.
   Summary: "Ted and Betsy Lewin detail the annual rescue of baby puffins by the children of Heimaey, the largest island in the Westman Islands off the coast of Iceland. Includes additional information about puffins and the Westman Islands, glossary, and further reading"—Provided by publisher.
   ISBN 978-1-60060-424-9 (hardcover : alk. paper)
1. Atlantic puffin—Infancy—Iceland—Heimaey (Westman Islands) 2. Wildlife rescue—Iceland—Heimaey (Westman Islands) I. Lewin, Betsy. II. Title.
QL696.C42L477 2012   598.3'3—dc23   2011032248